DISNEY HITS

ISBN 978-1-4950-5510-2

HAL•LEONARD®
CORPORATION

7777 W. BLUEMOUND RD. P.O. BOX 13819 MILWAUKEE, WI 53213

In Australia Contact:
Hal Leonard Australia Pty. Ltd.
4 Lentara Court
Cheltenham, Victoria, 3192 Australia
Email: ausadmin@halleonard.com.au

Visit Hal Leonard Online at
www.halleonard.com

CONTENTS

Bundle of Joy

Music by Michael Giacchino

The soundtrack to 2015's *Inside Out* was written by Michael Giacchino, who has composed the music for several other Disney/Pixar films, including *Up* and *Ratatouille*. The film follows the story of a young girl growing up, from the viewpoint of personifications of the emotions in her head: Joy, Fear, Anger, Disgust, and Sadness. "Bundle Of Joy" is a simple and effective piano-based piece featured early in the film.

Hints & Tips: Play the left-hand eighth notes with a rocking motion to keep them even and steady. This piece should be quiet throughout.

Almost There

Words and Music by
Randy Newman

This uplifting song from Disney's 2009 film *The Princess And The Frog* was composed by long-term collaborator Randy Newman and performed solo by actress Anika Noni Rose. The song describes how Tiana is so close to reaching her dream of opening her own restaurant, and proved so successful it was nominated for the Best Original Song Oscar, as well as being released in 41 different languages!

Hints & Tips: Be on the lookout for accidentals, as they crop up frequently throughout. This should be played with confidence, so break it down and practice in sections.

Just___ do-ing what I do.___ Look out boys,__ I'm com-ing through.__ And I'm

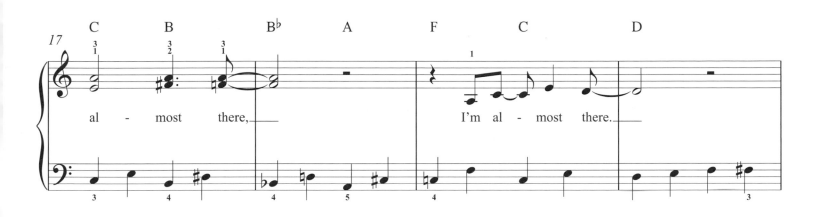

al - most there,___ I'm al - most there.

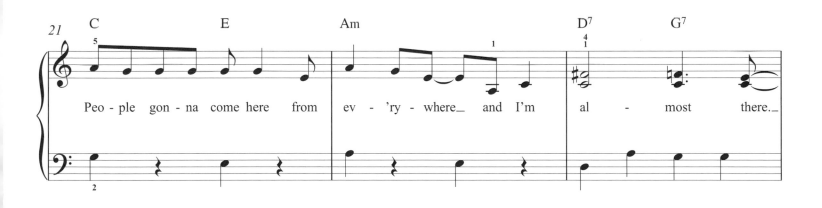

Peo - ple gon - na come here from ev - 'ry - where__ and I'm al - most there.__

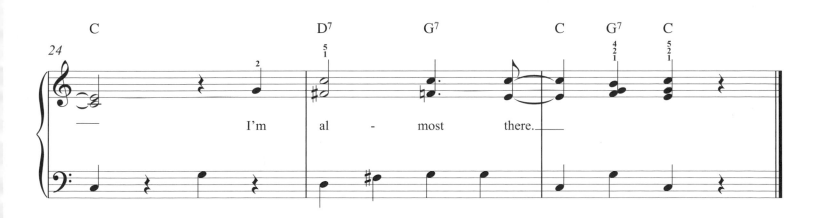

I'm al - most there.__

Be Our Guest

Words by Howard Ashman
Music by Alan Menken

Consistently rated by critics and Disney fans as one of the greatest songs from any Disney film, "Be Our Guest" was originally sung by Jerry Orbach, as the singing candelabra Lumière, and Angela Lansbury, as Mrs Potts. Composed by Alan Menken with lyrics by Howard Ashman, nearly every aspect of this true showstopper has been acclaimed, from the vocal performances and catchiness to the use of computer-generated imagery during its sequence in the film.

Hints & Tips: Note the time signature; it means you need to count two half notes per bar. Make sure you leave the full one-beat count for the quarter rests in the left hand.

Bouncy ♩ = 112

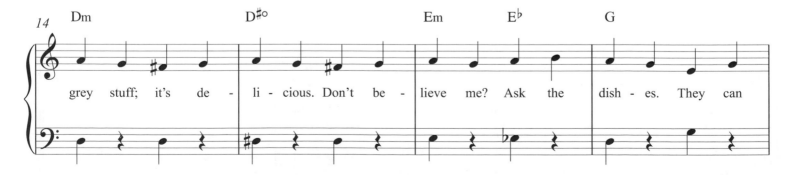

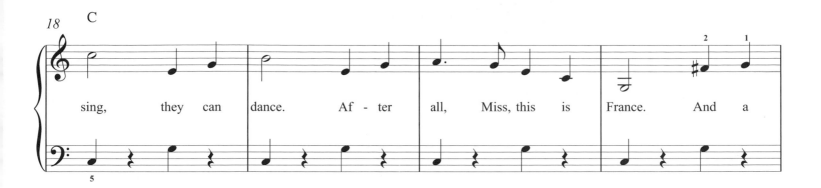

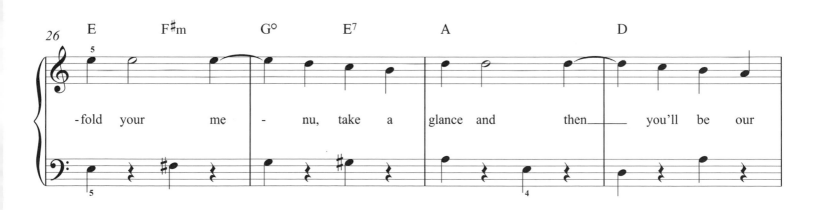

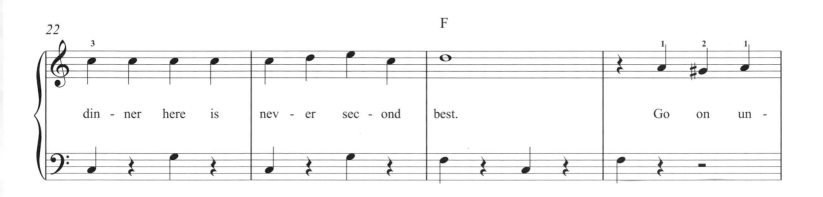

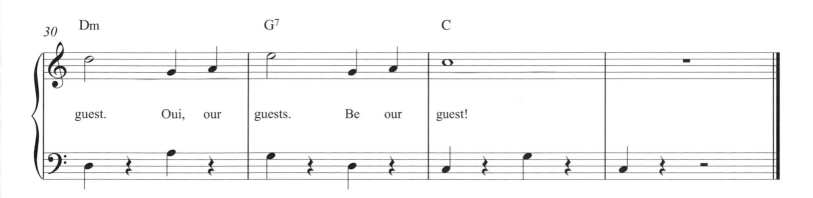

Down to Earth

Words by Peter Gabriel
Music by Peter Gabriel and Thomas Newman

Composer Thomas Newman and director Andrew Stanton enlisted singer and songwriter Peter Gabriel to perform the end-credits song for this blockbuster film about a waste-disposal robot. Gabriel is one of Stanton's favorite musicians, and Newman flew to London to compose this rousing anthem about environmental problems and our effect on the world – the principal themes of the film.

Hints & Tips: Start off softly at the beginning, so that there's a real contrast with the *forte* in bar 24. Note that the piece also changes key in bar 25.

A Dream Is a Wish Your Heart Makes

Words and Music by Mack David,
Al Hoffman & Jerry Livingston

This song was originally composed for the 1950 animated Disney film *Cinderella*, but this version was recorded by star Lily James for the 2015 live-action film's soundtrack. One of the most popular Disney songs, the tune features a wonderful melody as Cinderella optimistically sings of dreams coming true. Composed by Mack David, Al Hoffman, and Jerry Livingston, the song was used over the end credits of Kenneth Branagh's film adaptation.

Hints & Tips: The melody is in the left hand throughout, so keep the right-hand chords soft to allow it to come through. Check the ledger lines from bar 25, working out the notes first and writing them in if you need to.

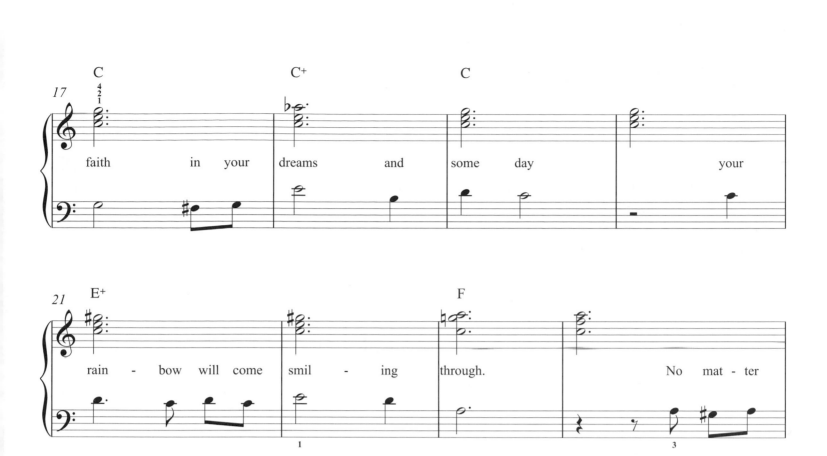

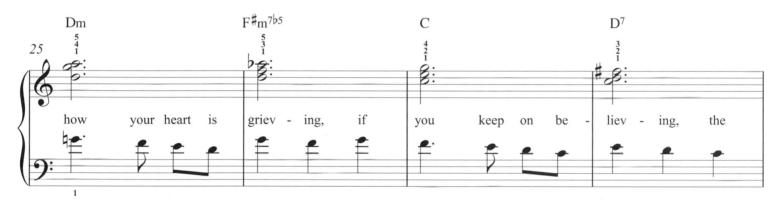

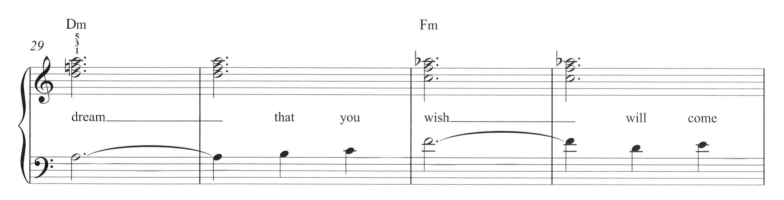

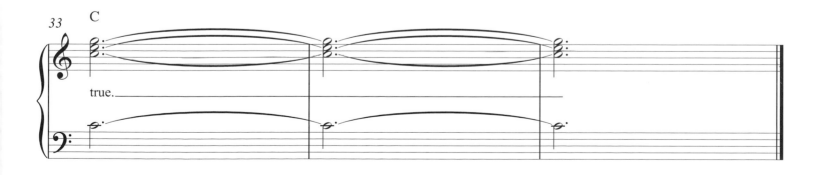

For the First Time in Forever

Words and Music by Robert Lopez
and Kristen Anderson-Lopez

Boasting excellent vocals from Kristen Bell (Anna) and Idina Menzel (Elsa), "For The First Time In Forever" tells the story of Anna's excitement when the gates are finally opened for Elsa's coronation. Elsa's part is a wonderful counterpoint melody that tells of her fear over accidentally revealing her powers. Filled with both seriousness and humor, the song features a line penned by the writers' daughter: "I wanna stuff some chocolate in my face."

Hints & Tips: Play through any difficult-looking rhythms before you begin, making sure you count carefully. Look out for 2/4 bar toward the end.

I Just Can't Wait to be King

Words by Tim Rice
Music by Elton John

One of five original songs written by Elton John and Tim Rice for the epic Disney classic *The Lion King*, "I Just Can't Wait To Be King" is an upbeat number sung by a young Simba along with Nala, a young female lion, and Zazu, a hornbill who works for the king's household. During the song, Simba expresses his feelings about growing up and all the things he's looking forward to when he becomes king of Pride Rock and no longer has to be bossed around.

Hints & Tips: Don't let the tempo drag in this bright, optimistic song. The use of accidentals means the Bs are sometimes flat and sometimes natural; be careful you don't get tripped up!

Rhythmic and bright (♩ = 80)

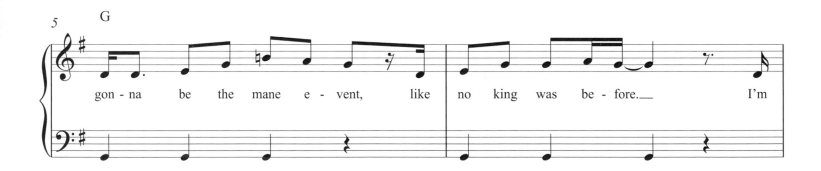

I Thought I Lost You

Words and Music by Jeffrey Steele
and Miley Cyrus

Sung by Miley Cyrus and John Travolta for the 2008 film *Bolt*, Miley Cyrus wrote this after the filmmakers asked her to write and sing a song with her co-star John Travolta. Travolta, who voices the dog Bolt, agreed to sing the song even before it was written, and heavily praised Cyrus's song-writing talents when it was finished. The song was nominated for a Golden Globe Award for Best Original Song.

Hints & Tips: Make sure the notes of the left-hand chords sound together; use these steady quarter notes to place the trickier right-hand rhythms.

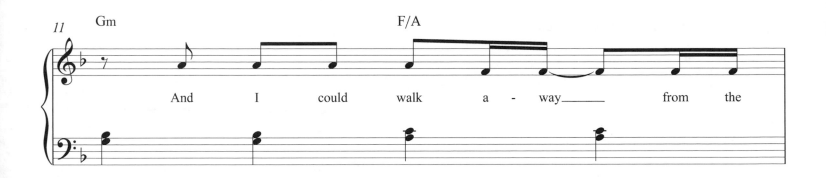

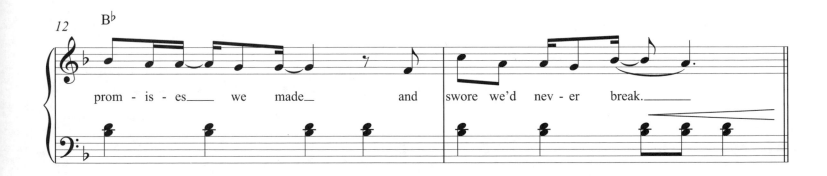

I See the Light

Words by Glenn Slater
Music by Alan Menken

This song was composed by Alan Menken, with lyrics by Glenn Slater, for Disney's 50th animated film *Tangled*. Performed by Mandy Moore and Zachary Levi, who played Rapunzel and Flynn Rider respectively, the ballad accompanies the "lantern scene" in the film, which was widely acclaimed by critics for the beauty of its animation. The sequence (and its 45,000 floating lanterns!) is remembered as the emotional peak of the film.

Hints & Tips: There are quite a few changes in position for the right hand, so check the fingering carefully. Play through bars 28 and 29 on their own, until you can play the eighth notes smoothly and in tempo.

Immortals

Words and Music by Peter Wentz,
Andrew Hurley, Joseph Trohman and Patrick Stump

When the rock band Fall Out Boy was approached to write a song for the soundtrack of 2014's *Big Hero 6*, they immediately understood the meaning of the film and wrote "Immortals." According to bassist Pete Wentz, the band liked the idea of the characters coming together to achieve something great, stating that they always identified with the underdog. The song plays over the end credits of the film.

Hints & Tips: There are lots of eighth notes and 16th notes to get your fingers round in this fast-paced song, but try to keep the movement going.

Let It Go

**Music and Lyrics by Kirsten Anderson-Lopez
and Robert Lopez**

"Let It Go," first heard in Disney's hit 2013 film *Frozen*, has since become one of the best-selling singles of all time. Composed by husband and wife songwriters Kristen Anderson-Lopez and Robert Lopez, the song was written for and originally performed by Idina Menzel, whose powerful singing perfectly voiced Elsa's newfound freedom. The song was reportedly composed in a single day, after an inspiring walk in New York's Prospect Park.

Hints & Tips: There's a lot to watch out for in this, so look through and mark in pencil anything you're unsure of. Practice these bits thoroughly before putting the whole piece together.

Lava

Words and Music by
James Ford Murphy

Lava is a short animated film that was featured at the start of Disney/Pixar's 2015 movie *Inside Out*. Written and directed by James Ford Murphy, the whole thing is a miniature musical love story, telling the tale of two volcanoes (Uku and Lele) falling in love over thousands of years. Sung with a simple ukulele accompaniment, "Lava" was released as a single in its own right and was featured as a bonus song on the *Inside Out* soundtrack.

Hints & Tips: Try playing with a metronome to help you with the differing rhythms. The left hand is repetitive, so get that perfected before fitting in the right.

Part of Your World

Words by Howard Ashman
Music by Alan Menken

Composed by Alan Menken with lyrics by Howard Ashman, "Part of Your World" was one of the first songs
in a Disney film that became known as the "I want" song, a big number that shares with the audience the
main character's hopes and dreams. To get a better idea of what Ariel would be feeling, singer Jodi Benson
requested that the studio's lights be dimmed to make her feel like she was underwater.

Hints & Tips: Make the whole song as expressive as you can, using the dynamics
and tempo markings to create an emotional performance.

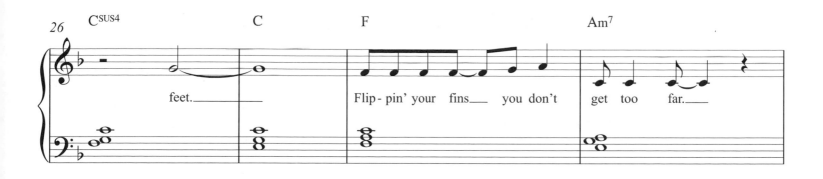

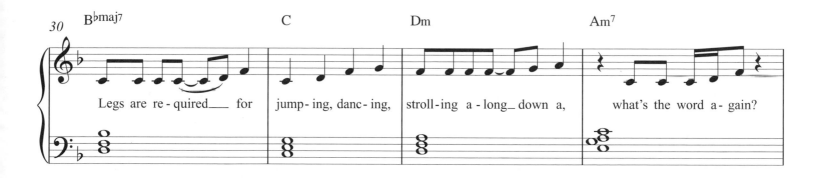

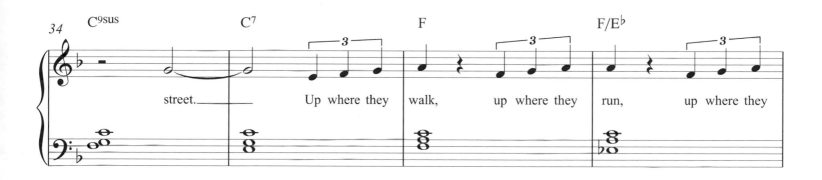

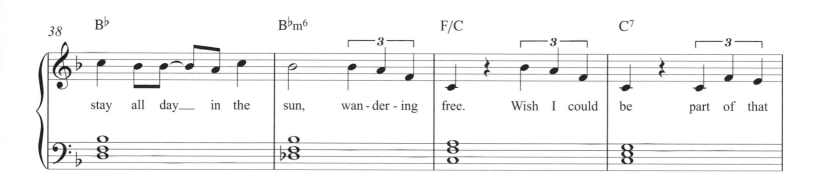

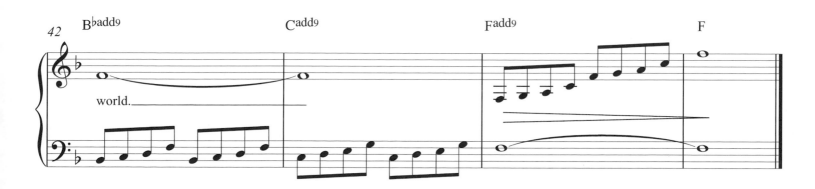

Once Upon a Dream

Words by Jack Lawrence
Music by Sammy Fain and Peter Tchaikovsky

The original "Once Upon a Dream" was featured in 1959's *Sleeping Beauty* and was based on a waltz from Tchaikovsky's ballet of the same name. Disney re-imagined this classic story in *Maleficent* and used a sombre, slow, and altogether darker cover of this song by Lana Del Rey. This version was much moodier and complemented the tone of the film brilliantly, helped by the unique vocal style of Del Rey, who was specially selected by lead actress Angelina Jolie.

Hints & Tips: Play this slowly with a haunted, dreamy feel; both hands should flow smoothly and evenly, and not plod along.

Reflection

Words by David Zippel
Music by Matthew Wilder

The 1998 film *Mulan* featured a performance of "Reflection" by actress Lea Salonga. It was also recorded by Christina Aguilera for the single version, becoming her debut single and propelling her to pop success. Aguilera was told she had to hit a specific note to be able to sing the song, so she reportedly practiced a Whitney Houston number for hours before hitting the note and getting the chance to sing the song.

Hints & Tips: While this starts in A major, there's a key change to C major early in the piece; however, there are still accidentals to watch out for.

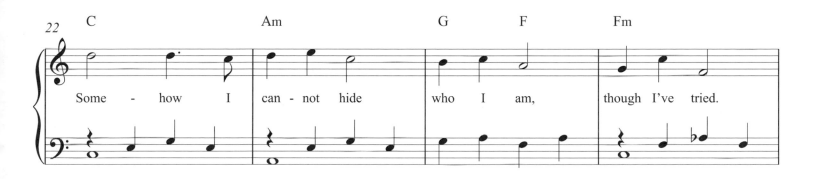

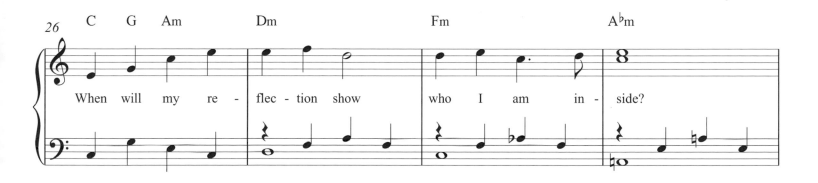

Shut Up and Drive

Words and Music by Peter Hook,
Evan Rogers, Carl Sturken, Bernard Sumner,
Stephen Morris and Gillian Gilbert

Used as part of the soundtrack for *Wreck-It Ralph*, Rihanna's 2007 tune has since become one of her most popular songs. Taking a sample from New Order's seminal track "Blue Monday," Rihanna's version tends toward a heavier pop-rock feel with overdriven guitars and a 21st century beat. The song marked Rihanna's fifth Top 5 single in the UK, its use in the film increasing its popularity.

Hints & Tips: Wherever the right hand plays more than one note at a time, make sure you play strongly so the notes sound exactly together.

Strong

Words and Music by Patrick Doyle,
Thomas Danvers and Kenneth Branagh

Composed by Patrick Doyle with Kenneth Branagh and Tommy Danvers, "Strong" was sung by Sonna Rele for the soundtrack of the 2015 version of *Cinderella*. The song has a modern R&B feel that mixes contemporary drum beats with a traditionally ballad-like vocal performance from London-based singer Rele. The song builds to an uplifting ending that reflects the emotions of the character by the end of the film.

Hints & Tips: While this song begins softly and slowly, it gains momentum in bar 25, where the rhythms get more interesting. Don't rush the first section or you'll find yourself tripping up when the rhythms become more complicated!

Heart-felt ballad ♩ = 138

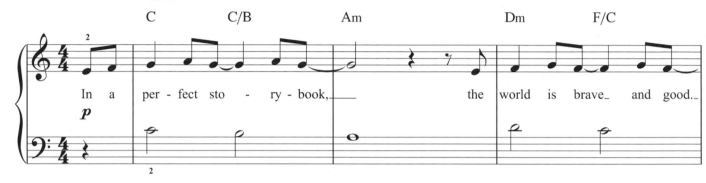

In a per - fect sto - ry-book, the world is brave and good.

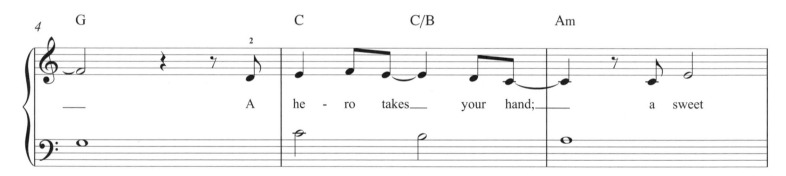

A he - ro takes your hand; a sweet

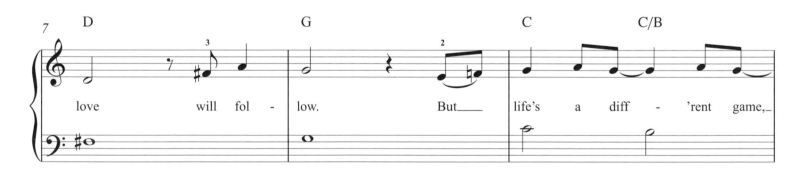

love will fol - low. But life's a diff - 'rent game,

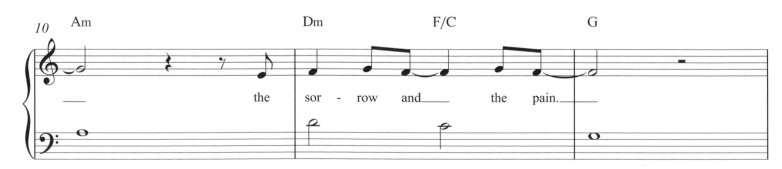

the sor - row and the pain.

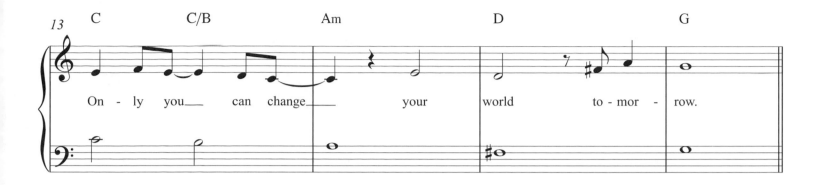

On - ly you__ can change__ your world to - mor - row.

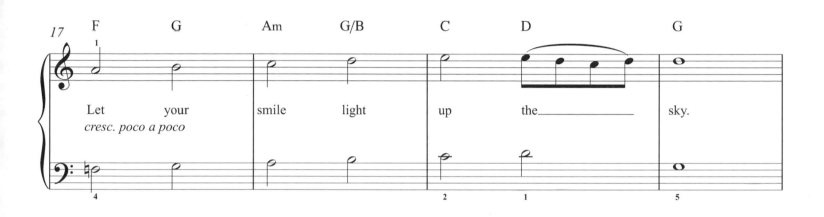

Let your smile light up the_____ sky.

cresc. poco a poco

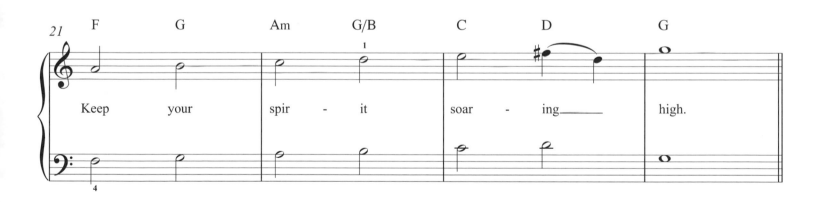

Keep your spir - it soar - ing__ high.

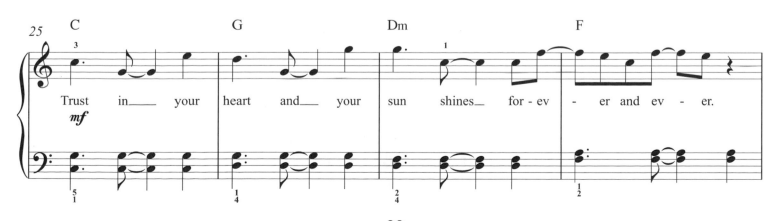

Trust in__ your heart and__ your sun shines__ for - ev - er and ev - er.

mf

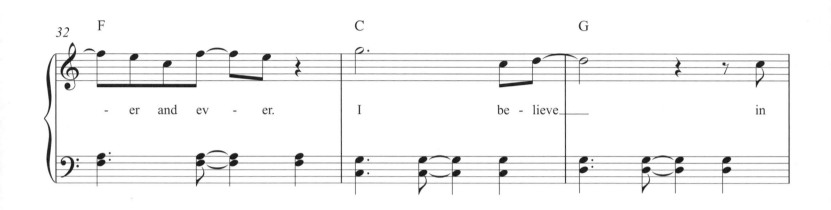

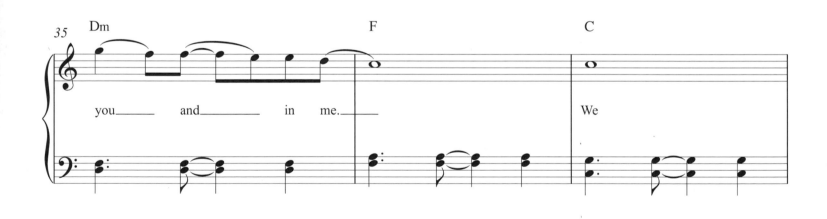

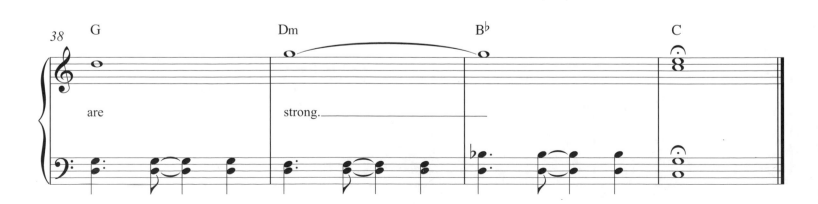

That's How You Know

Words by Stephen Schwartz
Music by Alan Menken

This song was composed for the soundtrack of *Enchanted* and, like the film, is an intentional homage to – and self-parody of – past famous Disney musical numbers. The music was composed by Alan Menken, who was perhaps the best man for the job since he also composed the music for many older Disney films. In the movie, Giselle (played by Amy Adams) sings to Robert (Patrick Dempsey) with help from a variety of people in Central Park, including buskers, dancers, and a steel band.

Hints & Tips: Practice each hand separately and slowly before trying them together at the correct tempo. Make the most of the left hand wherever it has a phrase that needs emphasizing.

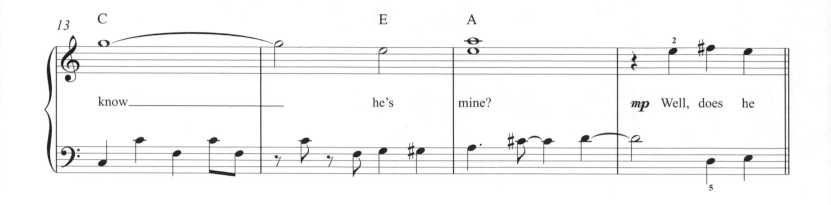

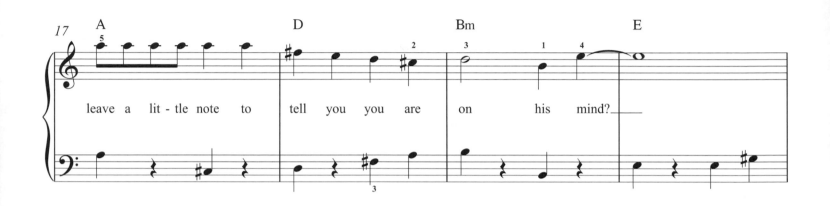

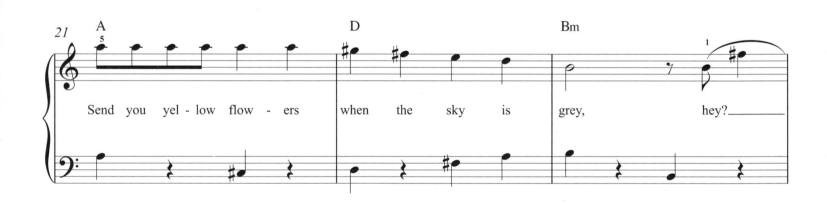

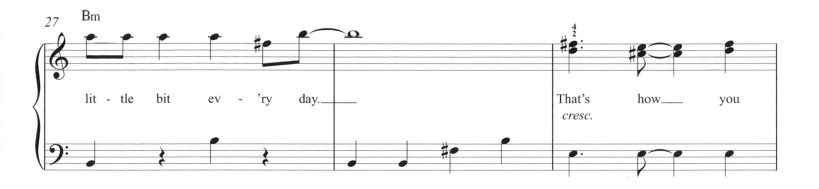

lit - tle bit ev - 'ry day._____ That's how___ you

cresc.

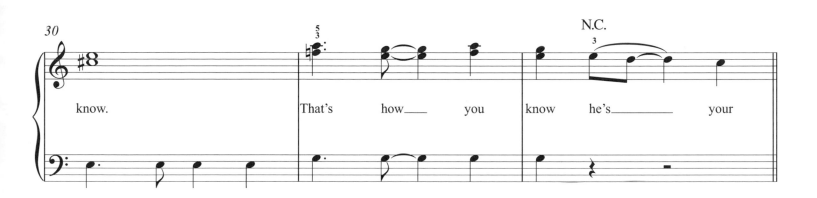

know. That's how___ you know he's_____ your

N.C.

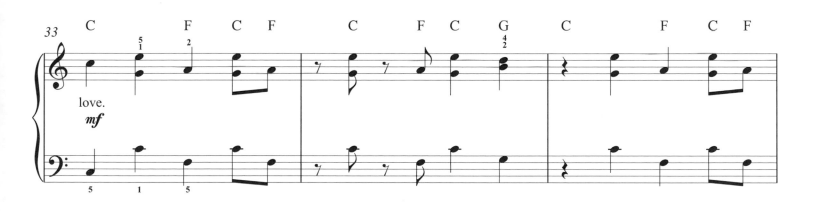

love.

mf

Touch the Sky

Words by Mark Andrews and Alexander Mandel
Music by Alexander Mandel

"Touch the Sky" is one of two original songs in *Brave* that were performed by Scottish-Gaelic singer Julie Fowlis. She is known for writing and singing in the language, and *Brave* was notable for being the first Disney film to feature it in the music. Her uplifting melody is backed by the driving rhythm of folk guitars and an array of traditional instruments, helping to enhance the Scottish Highland setting.

Hints & Tips: As this is such a fast piece, it would be a good idea to practice with a metronome, starting off slowly and building up to the correct tempo.

We Belong Together

Words and Music by
Randy Newman

Randy Newman wrote this fantastically enjoyable tune for the soundtrack of *Toy Story 3*, released in 2010.
Newman had previously composed music for the first two installments of the trilogy, earning huge acclaim from
audiences and critics alike. "We Belong Together" won the Academy Award for Best Original Song, only the
singer-songwriter's second song to win the Oscar, despite having received over twenty nominations.

Hints & Tips: This is rather a tricky piece. Break it down into separate hands, and then into sections,
and practice each bit on its own until you're really confident with it.